For C,
a fellow [...]
It works somehow.

Brian
AWP
2024

# Torch Lake

## & OTHER POEMS

BRIAN JOHNSON

# Torch Lake

## & OTHER POEMS

)•) Del Sol Press   Washington, D.C.   2008

Poems in this book, sometimes with different titles, appeared in the following publications: *The Alembic:* "Self-Portrait with Thunderbird," "Self-Portrait in the Tub, or Gloxinia"; *American Letters & Commentary:* "The Fig Trees of Italy," "Self-Portrait in front of Equestrian Statue"; *Barnabe Mountain Review:* "doorway for the house"; *Connecticut Review:* "Self-Portrait in Green"; *Flights:* "Boy on Stilts"; *Key Satchel:* "Self-Portrait with Red Gravy and White Gown"; *PP/FF: An Anthology:* "Self-Portrait with Apologia"; *Quarter after Eight:* "Self-Portrait with Magpie," "Self-Portrait at Torch Lake," "Self-Portrait as a Grand Hotel"; *Red Brick Review:* "Self-Portrait after Two Deaths"; *Self-Portrait* (a chapbook from Quale Press): "Self-Portrait with Magpie," "Self-Portrait with Lemon Tree," "Self-Portrait at the Construction Site," "Self-Portrait with Spire"; *Sentence:* "The Jar"; *The Styles:* "Self-Portrait as Egg White"; *Wavelength:* "Self-Portrait at the Smithy"; *West Branch:* "Self-Portrait (Little)," "Self-Portrait (Unhorsed)," "Self-Portrait in a Nebraska Bakery."

I would like to thank the Connecticut Commission on the Arts and the Connecticut State University System for grants that aided in the completion of this book.

I would also like to thank my mother, Diane, for believing in me through many winters and a lot of table-waiting.

Del Sol Press, Washington, D.C.
http://www.delsolpress.org

Paper ISBN: 978-1-934832-07-3

First Edition

Cover painting: Burghard Müller-Dannhausen, "Juli 1993 1." Acrylic on canvas.
http://www.mueller-dannhausen.com

Design & composition by Jonathan Weinert
http://www.jonathanweinert.net

Publication by Del Sol Press/Web del Sol Association, a not-for-profit corporation under section 501(c)(3) of the United States Internal Revenue Code.

*for Amy*

# CONTENTS

# PART ONE

## Still Life with Reptile and Dog

My unheavenly body moves toward the water, but it takes the whole day.

I'm different from the winged insects and the loud, bounding mammals that populate the earth. My father told me, "A reptile is a post. The world is a horsetail. Hold your ground."

And I do. My years are numbered; my mornings without incident; my afternoons long, hot, and solitary.

A dog guards the vast boneyard. I see it.

## Child Prodigy

My country was greener and hotter than Eden, and Eden must have been very hot, what with its fruit trees and all manner of inimical plants. Greener than Eden itself, my homeland, and teeming with bicycles in a sunlight you can only imagine. I was sitting pretty, yes I was. There was blood of course, but it flowed into the waterways and became part of the water. We drank without hesitation. There was a lot of drinking, partly because it was very hot and partly because we enjoyed it. It so happened that when the park overflowed with rioters, I sat there. It also happened that when the cars burst into flames, I sat there. Things were happening, and I couldn't do nothing, and yet what really could be done? I got money for my lost teeth. For my poetry I received none.

## Postcard: Patio in Nice

The magpie holds a paper hat I left overnight. She looks concerned, as birds often do, and walks nervously around bits of cake. I am doomed, even in the morning with her intimate and friendly eyes. I lean on the railing and watch the sea. It is a heavy curtain.

Pictures of saints, folded hands, already bathed in light. The following year bathed in light. Pink garments of Christ. When I was ten, I believed. He walked on the waves, he turned fish into bread, he made the holidays. The family ghost swept across the background, hanging from a chain.

I watch the sea undulate, brush itself, dissolve. I am her influence, like a painter after a second visit to France. Around nine, the magpie flies away. Only a few years earlier, the magpie was a robin. But this is worldly splendor: no one signs and dates their costumes, least of all a man.

## "I Wrote a Letter a Day . . ."

I.

I wrote a letter a day, hoping to find a place in someone.
I wrote in clothes and out of clothes.
I filled my envelopes with wild gestures, flocks of hair, shortbread.

II.

My native soil changed colors, and the family sofa burned.

III.

Shining cars with white flags passed through the hillside.
The animals had long ears, all of them.
They stared at me, me alone.

IV.

I shook at each rise in temperature.
There were red-barked trees, and blue-faced girls.

V.

The sky was slow, almost statuesque.

VI.

I filled my eyes with pure gestures, locks of hair, patterns.

VII.

*One must respect black,* I thought. *Nothing prostitutes it.*

## After Bosch

It appeals to my native tongue: not the plate, but the Hieronymussian gravy.

If I return to my fairytale—about old, deep-seated fears—the forest, the windmill—the massacre of innocents—I engage in all of it: eating, drinking, dancing, jumping, making love at a gallop . . .

And the frog, the frog never leaves my pail.

## Self-Portrait in Green

First it was a green bed, then a pair of six-foot green bookcases, and a green headdress. When I sat down to write each morning, I wrote with a green pen. Not only the ink, but the pen. I became green from the ground up, as green as the lumber—if not greener. It was my dream. The pieces were all green. And when I found the box of green sun, my white sun went into hiding. I could no longer breathe without green, the green could no longer breathe without me. Together we formed this strange valley, looking west, to those pinnacled hills. . . .

## October

I.

The land nearly at peace: barns silent, harrows in place.

II.

Sky heavier, and more austere.

III.

Roads with a colder look. Roads before men.

IV.

Old pick-ups—hoodless, windowless—waiting for the rain.

V.

Beer-colored grass. The wind nudging a dirty tablecloth.

VI.

A child wide-eyed with a sign: FRESH VEGES.

VII.

Homecoming: the leaves turn a red-orange.

VIII.

The big smoke from chimneys—late afternoon, sky a flawless blue—
fleeting.

IX.

Bodies, feet, under the moon-white silos.


X.

The wind advancing. And no one looking.

# Elements of a Story

Sky, and monster, and mistletoe, and squirrels.

Jack sees the mistletoe.

Two squirrels run off with a monster.

How beautiful is the peeled sky!

Doorways smell the world.

## Family Portraits

Families have the look of handmade toys. Dutch families are made of cork. British families are made of pipe cleaners. German families are made of sealing wax. Italian families are made of stick-pins. When those families cross the ocean, they become American, and American families are made of wood. Their wood is of two kinds: painted or untreated. In either case, the wood cracks. And then, the national humidity leads to warping: fathers and daughters split, sons turn to driftwood, and mothers turn to flat-bottomed boats. No one can stop it. Still, the pieces stay in place, as if the toymaker were controlling their fates. You see these wooden families at the movies. You see them at amusement parks. You see them wearing odd, brightly-colored outfits and standing on lawns. Their woodenness is so obvious, at times, that you'd almost prefer knocking and pounding them to caressing them. Then again, you are struck by the superior blank-faced solidity of the American family. Surrounded by their great dollhouses, the Americans seem immovable on the world stage, just as the Dutch seem resilient, the Brits eccentric, the Germans circumspect, and the Italians lively. You might wish that American families had a different character—more subtle, perhaps—but their simple and heroic materiality cannot be topped. When you're content to merely stare at them, and look no further, the soul of wood is irresistible.

## Torch Lake

I see a birdbath here, but no birds; a bottle of rum, but no drinkers; a piano, but no family.

These days all look the same: voiceless, headless. I am tempted to walk out, but no one would call after me, "Come back or else!"

So I stare at the water-rings and listen to the crickets.

Thy kingdom.

# PART TWO

---

*"He Lived in Exile for Many Years . . ."*

## 1. *The Garret*

I breathe convulsively. I labor. A chapter a day for three days, then nothing till Sunday. Always the same food—eggs, toast, soup—and the half-washed plate and cracked bowl.

No visitors except for R——.

For twelve years I have lived this way, thinking of myself and the city, wondering who is dirtier, more full of echoes, more disappointed. Someone is always on the stairs, and in the street.

I can't think of a first sentence. I can't think of them.

## II. *Mexico*

One never gets used to the dust: dust on hubcaps, on windshields, on boots polished just before walking out. And then the heat makes you slow as a turtle, and you drink to stay that way and suppress the moon that used to enchant you, a few years ago. Stray dogs and laughing kids make you think that your moment has gone, and it has.

You'll die without trees.

III. *Transfigured Night*

The stars are selfless, radiant but impersonal, never moving from their first position. They draw me up to the roof—I remove my shirt and lie back. If only love were an offspring of mathematics, and the stars a sumptuous nowhere with terraces in the heart.

## IV. *Found in Italy*

Found in Italy,
which for him was a religious act.

He sat on a rock,
leaning forward,
as if playing ball,
which for him was good.

The most beautiful and accurate of all dreams
lightly touched the rock
he stood on.

It was the beginning—
alone, which for him is a religious act,
with locusts and with honey.

## v. *Miles*

As I move again, the landscape continues to elude me. I would graze in this meadow, but where are the goats? I would carve my signature in a trunk, but where is the nymph or the piteous memory? I search vainly for an episode of war, a moment of awe, a visitation at dusk, something to convince me that I am the lone romantic hero embarking on a quest. Instead I spend my day wandering, meandering, not quite banished, but slowed by an ever-growing sadness, a confidence, of sorts, that abrupt changes and new conquests are not in store for me. I've come to ignore the ships lying in the bay, and I look half-vacantly at the dandelions and volcanic cones. This landscape is the work of a copyist.

## VI. *At Some Point*

The fine-spun theories of resistance get reduced to ash: one tires of holding out, of writing long, unforgettable letters, of avoiding the crowds and the television and family dinners. Solitude becomes prosaic, not the uncollared terrifying animal with its own sound.

At some point, I will take your hand, remove your beaver hat & pearls, and throw you into my world.

## VII. *Olive Drab*

Abroad, a fleet of colors greets me—

| | |
|---|---|
| Pale Blue | Royal Blue |
| Emerald Green | Ruby Red |
| Plum | Violet |
| Mahogany | Snow White |
| Chocolate | Lemon |
| Sea Green | Gold |
| Cardinal | Oyster |

*I see Diana in her emerald green slip; the lemon ice at Pepé's; a spoon of lemon juice; lemon meringue pie, which my grandfather's father called lemon syringe pie; lemon drops, and the lemon tree at my cousin's in Florida; their sea-green bathroom; Dorothy's slippers; the Vatican, and Luther's war on indulgence; the seven hills of Rome, the seven dwarfs; Gainesborough's Blue Boy; also Kind of Blue and Sketches of Spain and Blue Note and Verve; the royal blue, double-breasted dress of a woman buying doughnuts; Besse Smith, and Billie Holiday who was beautiful in her youth, and my dream of sleeping with a blues singer; the other blues, ultramarine and sapphire: the heavily pigmented, deeply faceted life, never pale or fading; and the plum-colored dessert at 512 Loring; the plum blossom spring of Hiroshige; the famous plums in the doctor's icebox, now completely eaten and written out; the plum job, the plum deal, held out and withheld, drawn up and withdrawn, the elusive sugarplums, the future; intermarriage, cross-breeding, the ecstatic trance, when surfaces present a different face, a violet, iridescent, bluish face, emotions being one insoluble family, one irresistible weight, moment on moment, a dark wood wandering, Friday night, Friday night as a twenty-year-old, with books,*

*books and women, women in and out of books, the dates arriving, departing, trespassing, the Kates, the Beatrices, no Beatrice, no Kate, but unexpected kisses and strange figures, cross-legged on their grandmother's quilt, and pantiless in their grandpa's mahogany chair; love on mahogany, the mahogany-dark air of those years, living with books, and leaving them, living and dead women, life and death intercourse, in snow, on grass, between printed sheets, a luxury, a heavy peace; heavy, sweet, dense, the chocolate rabbit that cannot hop, the dark chocolate soil that lines the river, still rabbit and dark soil and heavy trees, but occasionally the gold leaves, the gold foil, a trick, the unbearable lightness of being; the box of gold foil at K-Mart; the golden dome of St. Peters; Hopkins and the god of shook foil; the golden tan of my cousin in Florida, under her lemon tree, unphotographed, sleeping, with her golden calves; the gold rushes and eggs of the mind, stored up for another day, for graduation day, when I lose my olive drab, and move house to the greater company.*

## VIII. *Neither Spread nor Rounded*

My poor body is based on geometry:
Perpendicular, stiff
Unhappy
At the end of its line.

Perfect is the stone
Of isolation.

How I would love
A theater-in-the-round,
A kidney-shaped pool
Somewhere to meet others
Instead
And be spirited.

I am a bust,
Cracked and flowered.

My poor body says no
And nothing more:
Perfect is the stone
Of isolation.

## IX. *Sliding Doors*

They open and close smoothly—almost imperceptibly—the air becoming glass, and the glass, air, whether the one between them wears a bathing suit or a raincoat, whether she is bearing fruit or hooded, they have a pleasing sound (swoosh coming out, swoosh going in), nothing abrupt or jarring, scornful, sudden, the violence and the blindness, the heaviness and fullness of wooden doors, for decades the code of architectural behavior, as sliding doors are the felony.

## x. *Paris*

The streets, gaslit at night, an infrastructure of drains and sewers hardly dimming their opera, and their jazz, a Babylon of well-dressed bodies mingling and shuffling, or stiffening with recognition of an old flame. In Paris, every neighborhood is popular to someone: the anatomy of its buildings, its shaded areas, comforting, or perhaps sad, like a singer from the old days who has gotten heavy, lost some range, and depends on our loyalty to seem beautiful.

These streets, even the boulevards, they have all grown up. They overthrow their own engineers; they despise their Gallic music; they need our motives to seem classic, and our smoky breath to seem romantic. The gas lamps support our ambition; looking up at them, who is not ready to be drawn out again, night by night, a humiliation in dense quarters, or a sail with an unprintable face?

## XI. *Paris in the Morning*

Rainy city.
Our Lady.
Dark.

Till the peacocks.

## XII. *The Dark Continent*

I have visited it.
Tar-pits.
Towers of mud.

People slept indoors. Fans blew.

No one spoke at that time.

The mothers had bottle-green eyes.

Some watched the discordant birds, the browning lakes.

The boy wore a steel-gray suit,
The girls had jet-black hair.

There were pig roasts every Friday,
and clubs where the people danced,
two of each breed,
till they all lay down,
polychromed and entranced.

Afterwards, people failed to describe it.
No words came to mind.

The fathers had brick-red lips.

Things befell the continent:
Strange, complex, seamy, unwritten.

I have visited it,
Myself and others.
Silence was a tax.
Silence was a sort of bleach.

## XIII. *Steer*

Which way? Which way to the ranch? Are you certain? Say it again. Do
I turn here? Is it more of a gradual veer? Will I pass any landmarks—
anything I know, that I can remember? Is this the quickest way? Should
I put on music? Do you play any games, any road-games? Roll down the
window, please, and I need to know: where you were born? Which exit
are we looking for? The birds: what are they talking about? And the stars:
what do they mean? Something I can write down, something I can know
and remember. When you comb your hair, what does your mind do? Do
you play any games, any road-games? Are we almost there? Please tell me
again. When did you make the tourniquet? When did you leave the land?
Which motive is most like a barrel?

## XIV. *Gold–Helmeted Face*

Your image—

Its lightly salted, deeply arched foot
Its small but buoyant, ripe but continent breast
Its familiar, gold-helmeted face—

In my stable, in the middle of the night.

## xv. *"He Sat Trifling with a Pen..."*

He sat trifling with a pen, full of echoes and yet scriptless now for many years. Chinese philosophers spoke of the ten-thousand things; the French novelist of the ten-thousand women he had slept with. For the French, the Chinese, all those wonderful—those partings of bushes—those flashes! Where was his ten thousand? Trifling, in despair, the poet sat there. An unseemly life, his, a sail with an unprintable face, a spotted wandering that brought him nothing, and took him noplace. Sometimes he could barely speak of it. A dense and grounded heart, his.

He adjusted his trifocals, and leveled his gaze, wearily, at the world outside. There was snow, and a woman, and the words "fall snow" and "tall woman." The snow blew around, thickly and randomly; the woman struggled with her hood; and he wrote and wrote about Eskimos, their firelight, their fur, their seventeen kinds of snow, until he was done, finally, with writing. A familiar emptiness settled in him and the room. There was Pound, mad, ancient, black-caped, found in Italy. And what about Rilke in his castle, or Crane dying on the way back from Mexico? Such thoughts troubled him, as if he were part—the worst part—of the yearly forecast. Suicide ran in his family; and depression, too, the heavy trees. December was all he knew. Once he put the pen away, he fell. The gulf was so deep, so violet, that only daylight could remove it.

## XVI. *Lisbon*

Loads of sunshine
in this country
Malaga grapes
packed in cork
a crowd
to stand on the pier
to watch me
deck-tall
on the incoming liner.

Malaga grapes
packed in cork
loads of sunshine
steep hills, white walls
I'm coming in
with oats, tin
a great quantity of wood
the soul of another country
young,
favorable for raising.

XVII. *Canals. Windmills.*

If we remember the Dutch people and their home, reclaimed from the sea. The absolute refusal of death. My grandmother at fifteen. The stiff-backed grace.

If we remember the harrowing of Rembrandt's face, and the harrowing of Van Gogh's, and later find some letters, some instruments, some young girls, some light, the beauty of Jan van der Meer van Delft's private life—

We must go on.

XVIII. *Far Inland...*

I became a huge recumbent form, as the sun opposed me. Fiercely. I said no. For three years I drank citric acid in the mornings and beer in the evenings, the bushes grew tall around me, the sun went away, and I became statuary. I turned white, a cool white, mindful of wind, mindful of the wind's fondling, and in continuous opposition to the sun, the sun whose clouds of dust and great magnified shadows move around the earth, building scenery at the expense of flesh.

XIX. *Mother,*

It is always summer in the flesh: the senses do nothing but fish and dream:
it is Florida as I remember it: tennis earlier in the day, before lunch, when
the air is still and cool, and the clay unprinted: the clay untouched except
by birds: when the heart is full, when the heart is lord and mother: lord in
the garden, mother at the baths.

## xx. *Lines Written on Grand St.*

And the stars are incapable of words, yet emit their pulses.

‡

Birdland: a gyroscope shadows the wheat.

‡

The bicycle spins down the hill. Riderless.

‡

So many holes yet to be played.

‡

Wandering, by a river in Germany.

‡

On my back, cloudlike markings. On my chest, polished knobs.

‡

The perfume is mistaken for spring, a name.

‡

All that is sacred: the empty lot, the face covered with mulch,
the moon floods.

‡

The world of gaslight and ironwork. This world.

‡

O loftiest of gulfs, magnified, a hallway . . .

‡

I bathed with the poet's family.

‡

The moon floods on. We prepare the hermitage.

‡

And youth is overthrown, tossed, into the leaf-speckled pool.

‡

A story tells itself.

‡

Waving, my toe on the step.

XXI. *In a green and pleasant land*

Among the blurred landscapes and foreshortened urns,
   I show up.
Among the rolling estates and smoking roofs,
   I seem ill-bred
   full of wonder
   American.

## XXII. *Bell, Distant*

*Few are the moonlit nights I've cared for.*
—SEFERIS

A sound wave emanating from St. Cecilia's or St. Mary's fills me with a longing to pray, and touch something, a chalice, a nape, an old map of Europe, some beautiful thing that needs the attention. My earthly life has grown indelicate, tone-deaf, like one of those great steel cities, busy all day and dead after six. I cannot tell the difference between dew and water, between the coloratura and the mezzo-soprano. Truth lies underneath the bricks, happiness is just beyond the ridge, and I would like to keep working. The sound holds me for a minute, only, during which the memory of prairie grasses, fireweed in bloom, mariposa lilies, and a potentilla leaf reasserts itself. It fills me with mist, the wish to go home, to go back home, to leave the great steel cities with their corridors and heavy doors, to find myself in the wilderness. But nostalgia, I think, is another form of self-absorption, no better than the one it replaces. Nature is for children, and saints and music too. They can't have me.

## XXIII. *Twentieth Century Music*

Armed forces of the Slavic
King Stravinksy.
Nothing feminine-waltzy.
Serrated edges. Sans serif type.

Strauss left Vienna
when Berg arrived
with his pale yellow skin
and sawlike teeth.

Bartok is a hayride
gone awry.
Nothing faint, pillowy,
but all sorts of needles.

One listens to it, dis-
enchanted, disturbed.

One eats the acid fruit.
One likes the exploded view.

## XXIV. *At the Equator*

"Every line is imaginary," said the natural scientist, "and so the boy standing on the line is also imaginary; this figment of earth is matched by his figment of flesh.

"He experiences extreme heat, extreme moisture, a chaos of fecundity and greenery so dense that the trees must grow to miraculous heights even to reach the sunlight. Some of the trees, like the wild rubber tree, assume fantastic and never-before-seen shapes. And the imaginary boy is struck by the intermingling of species in the undergrowth and canopy. There are no straight lines in nature, no this half of the bed and that half of the bed—in short, no divisions. The man with erect military posture, perpendicular to the earth, drawing the line with extreme care, that man is the boy's father and so exists for the boy, though we know both are fictional and as imaginatively fixed as the line.

"All three (boy, man, line) remain subject to evaporation (they can be forgotten), but they already have a habitation and a name. The boy and the man are from Michigan, while the equator—sometimes called the celestial equator—is a part of all the books on geography and astronomy. To stand on this line is to feel the hottest place on earth: hot, wet, and evergreen."

## xxv. *A Race*

I knew my race, but I feared yours. The locker room was tense. You had the bigger dicks and the better music and the warmer mothers. I knew it. We had the better diction and the bigger houses. You knew it. Everyone was civil, very civil, to the point of friendliness. We were all self-possessed. Was it hatred? No. More like fascination, which is a cause and effect of separation, in time. I want to approach, but dare not. When I try to run out of myself, I run into myself. The same for you, I suspect. All this running gets us nowhere: it makes a man into a roadside dog, trembling, of mixed parentage.

## XXVI. *Cardinal Points*

*North*
Where the invisible becomes visible
The air is thin.
Thy breath, shapely.

*South*
I am worn out
In the earth's crust
Holding an old firearm.

*West*
A region of canyons and squinting men.
The rock faces the rivers of sand.
A zero-sum game.

*East*
O would-be spring
Colorful measures
On a motionless head.

XXVII. *In the Vicinity of Ruins*

—the dense, deaf-mute populations; the impregnable marble and Pythagorean silences; the weed-eaten steps, the former baths thick with algae, the half-missing fresco and half-finished mosaics; the home burials and crumbling urns, the evidence of vile custom, tales, appetites—the places of civilized plunder and slow repossession.

I am their governor now, and their friend.

# PART THREE

## Artifact

The hands lie in a purer sphere. They float among waters, and women's hair, detached from their business.

When he said, "Here is the plan of my castle," his hands were already thinning, already skeletal and fey . . .

But he wanted to build his castle. They understood him, and came clawing up his wrists, and flexed their digitalia.

They continue to grow, searching for bits of a puzzle, for the final piece—corner—limb—

Where a tinker lives, a tinsmith.

# Before Rising

I lay straight and still upon my bed.

And see it all, everything: the clock paperweight and the fishtail candlestick—the spackled line in the ceiling—the thesaurus without a spine—the yellow phone—the used hatbox that needs a top.

The world has experienced me.

I need two windows: one window to bring light, and another to bring tongues.

## Boy on Stilts

I keep up with the voyages of discovery. That is, I see the way towns and ships are sprinkled over a map. I note the way flesh is executed on a canvas. I understand both the fall of the Roman Empire and the girl on Watteau's swing.

I've developed a taste for apples, which I pluck from the highest branches with care, like a great-grandmother plucking roses from her favorite rosebush. Orpheus is skeptical of me, but when I tap his burned shoulder, he relents and gives me the lute.

One night, unexpectedly, I stumble upon my lost father. He doesn't see me, but recognizes my voice from childhood. He says, "Where are you going?" And I say, "Home." I continue walking the other way, wondering if he is drunk, or if I am happy.

## My Apartment, My Sadness

When I return to it, when I return to my seat, alone, with a view of two rooms, mine and theirs, her pacing, him staggering and crying, all of us ready to talk, I pause—and, spreading the wings of a paperback in my lap—I consider how my life is spent, devouring novel after novel, ignoring the clock, ignoring bedtime and worktime, for the simple joy of finishing it, then raising the Venetian blinds and considering the lagoon, a couple in a gondola, a square, and all the rest, familiar from earlier scenes, in other novels, novels about characters in search of a home, a more beautiful spot, free of wounds, where the foxgloves bloom and the inhabitants stay, where conditions rarely vary from the ideal, which is unearthly: to be left inside, to be left outside, to be childless, to be penniless, are earthly states, acceptable, pleasurable, as long as some afternoon light falls, and the orange peels, and a can grows warm on the seat-arm, while I feel the pivotal moment: a woman who speaks for her sex, such beautiful letters, she comes to ruin, she comes to the unthinkable act, the final movement of a day, all afternoon, all morning, a night lying up in bed, eager for it to happen, savoring the inevitable break, knowing the novelist has prepared me, but has not prepared me, and so what happens next will not be realistic, or romantic, or tragic, or witty, but disturbing in a way I cannot understand, trapped as I am in my life, in my apartment and my sadness, which can take no further turns for the worse, as in a novel when the main character has passed through the stages of inner turmoil only to enter the stage of complete desolation, for which the only solutions are the monastery or death, a final retreat or a final advance, to put it in terms of warfare, for I can see that this love, like all loves beginning in perfect harmony, will end on a strange and unfathomable note, denying the possibility of a future, a still-higher music, such as the birds make in their feeders and dead-tree nests, first thing in the morning, before I've even splashed my face and kissed the picture, who will soon become my wife, not knowing the worst about me, for I expect a violent end, in which I stand making breakfast, not answering the phone and not looking for work, crying over the scrambled eggs, ruined as easily by life as I was ruined by famous authors and their stories of affairs, written in the third person, omniscient, as if that increased their wisdom, as if that put things in the proper perspective, all the crying, the staggering characters returned to their box, the oil and blood dried up, the author's hands cleanly withdrawn, leaving the reader, me, the first person in the empty room, raising the Venetian blinds, returning the paperback to its place, staring at the untouched rows, far hungrier than I ever thought possible, and far heavier.

## Picnic Rest

The countryside. Rushes and grass. Birdsongs. So we sit up, enjoy it. I pour the margaritas. You smile and recite the old verses. Beauty comes to dominate our mood, and how beautiful it is, the craggy hills surrounding our bedspread.

Then comes the shade, a time-elapsed drapery that moves without moving. You sit like a tiny statue on the grass. Nature, instantly still, registers our mood. Crickets regale and bore us. As do leaf-colors and leaf-notes. The river is darker; the moon bigger, and steadier.

These forms lying on a rock. This moonbathed scene. Admiring the lights of the Thunderbird, I think of you. In boots and a raincoat, furious, one of the great baroque masterpieces. How can I say such things? Are you not the muse? I know. A broken trumpet does not lie.

## After Two Deaths

I shall never wear the toga, or carry the staff, or marry Xanthippe, or teach in a homely way.

Nor can I imitate Christ. To be full of Christ is harder than to be philosophical, though both are very hard.

One must be ready to sit under the pine-trees at noon, with a few prayers, waiting for night and the unflickering truth.

## The Tub, or Gloxinia

The tub is seven feet long, bone white, and shifts and rocks in the sand as a midsummer wind comes off the bay. The warm, foam-crowned waters of the tub, where no one can reach me, where I close my eyes to the disciplined world of my father, grow cooler as my kids and their ships and sandcastles drift away, barely noticing my failures. I should be at my desk, writing, but the poem that I loved Friday, that described the deer and the poplar in one word, fills me with shame on Saturday. So it must go on like this, the work and the uncertainty, until I am no longer conscious, or conscious in a way that eliminates all the statues from the world, and all the battles. Then I will find Gloxinia, the muse of water, who sleeps on a bed of pennies and changes her body, at sunrise, from violet to postal blue. Then I can stop crushing my body and my youth, and love Gloxinia. Her game is silence, the silence a one-legged heron orchestrates for the moon. The silence of the reeds and the fog and the woodland snow. The silence I can never possess, though I write until my hair turns silver and no one recognizes me, not even my son. As I close my eyes, I feel the skyline and Gloxinia's endless sheets of rain.

## Long Wet Hair

The conspiracies of heaven find me in the park, where I am waiting for something else to happen, for a woman in white shorts and a polka dot shirt knotted under her breasts to approach me and take my hand, the way that women take your hand, half-openly, half-secretly, suggesting a happiness that is already present yet still in hiding.

While we are waiting for them, nothing else in the world matters, not the books we were reading, nor the fountain pen that fell in the grass, nor the work we've put off another day. We are the complete slaves of memory, and of the childish pictures it keeps. Behind the screen door she looms, with her knot and her long wet hair.

Years later, I walk up the sidewalk and open the door. She whispers to me in a pure voice, her vowels clearer and sweeter than anything on earth, more moving than Verdi. Now the two of us listen to Verdi, raptly, in the bedroom. Our gestures are half-imagined, and crystallize long before we complete them. Sometimes I untie the knot. Sometimes she does.

I sit here, almost happy, with a lemon tree at dusk.

# Synopsis of Nights

Lovemaking has worn me to a shadow.

My forehead is hot and full of stars.

Billie Holiday fills up the night.

I wish I could sing. I feel like singing.

The crickets have never been more insistent.

I stand by the window, listening, naked from the waist down.

## Self-Portrait in Jar

I've nothing to hide. I was a toad before. Now I'm a frog, and soon I will be a butterfly. An hour in the jar changed my heart.

I was a man before—I will not become a man again, lie down in darkness, tell stories. Only yesterday, I wore you out with lies. Now the bedroom is rid of me, the woods are rid of me, the road is rid of me.

I've nowhere to go. A fetus is revolving in your hands, before your very eyes.

Good night, says the fetus.

# Annaemmacharlotte

I am myself in bed, with no words, without a future.

Gone is the world of my Russian novel, with its drunks and its hunting scenes; my French novel with its ruinous courtships; my British novel with its money-plots.

I stay up late, thinking:

All the ornaments on the tree; after-school games; summer camp and music lessons; the long drive to the coast. . . .

What a sandbox, a fib, the heart is.

# The Fig-Trees of Italy

Sadly, and so like a man, jumping from one square to the next, I can see you, but I can't express it. An awful lot of young partridges and young doves will say it.

That's what I can't say, what I want to say.

You have the cambala annulata, the Kyrie eleison. I can say the names. It's the words that bother me. Better without words. Better with my eyes closed. And the windows open.

In the early summer among the fig-trees of Italy.

# The Palace at 4 a.m.

Rubens was fine, and rich, but Giacometti is my father.

My hold on reality is shaky, like his, and metaphysical, somewhere between the old men in French cafés and the ghostly lines in children's drawings. And I have trouble sustaining my appearance: my clothes are always outgrowing me. Remember Prospero in *The Tempest?* All that is solid melts into air? Prospero was Giacometti's stepfather, as surely as I am Giacometti's son. Like him, I rarely leave my studio country. My bones lose their volume; my face loses color. I am grown shadowy, and don't recognize my country or my queen. So must the king awake from his dream, only to find the austerity of light and the expiration of flesh too much to bear. And the king goes mad, and refuses to bathe or walk, but presses the window with long fingers, or his nose. He stares wildly at the bed—a family obsession. And look at his ankles,—how thin, how hairless they are!—the family ankles.

Albert Giacometti is my father, but all his dogs and wheels and halfmoons, his 4 a.m. palaces, they're with him.

I am the last monkey.

## Through the Slats

One in every city: a holy spear, pointed at the firmament. Whether I'm here to peel a hard-boiled egg, or to stand in the winter light and rub my shoulders dry, or to lose myself in the oak trees with Johannes Brahms, I am facing it.

On this intensely blue afternoon, when hair colors and bare arms flash in the street, the spire demands that I look up. Granite, austere, it points but never shakes: it gleams with a great cleanliness: it reproaches me calmly. It is self-possessed, unlike myself.

Mine is the tragedy of being various, glancing at more than one woman, and experiencing more than one desire: I am the restless, secretive kind. I can't wait to be somewhere pure, in another photograph, in a different world, with the wooden slats behind me.

## Bread and Circus

I.

"It is a lunar, rain-filled season!" I cried.

"Look at all that grass!" I shouted, "Look at all those pastries!"

"There is a symphony in the trunk," I said.

II.

My arm smelled like burnt almonds, then like gingerbread and cedar.

The sky widened to a final complexion.

The plains turned a strangely rich rose, and I, too.

## In front of Equestrian Statue

This morning I am a conqueror, a prince. I have presence of mind. The sheet is my valet. When subjects knock, the sheet says, "Please wait outside," or "Your appointment is canceled." No one objects. I return by and by to the sacred wood.

A little German waits for me, and the ballerina from Poland.

## Self-Portrait at Ethan Allen

The highbacked chairs like my company. They want their legs caressed, their cushions plumped. The floral couch is beckoning, too. It holds a full-length nude, awake, her chest rising and falling with Grecian ease, her thighs opening and closing in the fluorescent night.

The imagination of man's heart is evil from his youth. I sit in my favorite chair—oxblood, lined with nails—and I survey my children, my hands, my heavy-eyed mistress. She loosens her robe. I loosen mine. She hangs on my words; her hair hangs on my parted lips . . . .

But I grow cold again. I grow restless. The highbacked chairs lose their distinction. And the couches hold no further mysteries. Why do I waste myself on these trips? How much of my misspent middle-age is left? Now I stand waiting, waiting, a horseman at the gate.

## Unhorsed

When the horse appears on the screen, running at half-speed, looking confused, you will know immediately, having viewed a similar scene in other Westerns, that I was thrown, perhaps after being shot, perhaps while descending a hill.

During the next scene, the camera pans to the bottom of a canyon, where I am, crawling in the dirt with a broken leg, looking for my water. The sun is unbearable. No one rides through this place. You understand that I may not survive, even until the next morning.

The camera returns again and again to a few images: the trail of blood, the damp shirtfront, the canyon wall. My horse fails to return. In this movie, I never find either water or goodness, but I redeem myself by dying with such courage, openly, in one take.

# Time for Motley

The prophets said, "There is a time for this kind of love, and a time for that. A time for The Magic Flute, a time for Deep Throat." If I mistake the time, please, stay with me. I am still a young man. You should never drop a young man, as you would never slap an old man. We are both confused, and confusion leads to curious fantasies, and curious fantasies to strange acts. Listen, please: I mistook my two loves. I mingled them, as one mingles Latin and Anglo Saxon in a graveyard. I am still as tall as ever, as muscular, as brilliant as you wish. And if I emerge a polished husband, the Viking still hangs in the closet, furry-as-a-dog, ready to shake at your command. Your man Monday is not your man Friday, and we're all a species of harebrained Lear, wandering the face of the earth, asking his subjects, "Who is it that can tell me who I am?" Melancholia always gives way to Saturnalia, and Saturnalia drives toward Bacchanalia, where the very concept of risk melts away. Still, by the end of the night, Melancholia is never quite dislodged. The most festive of operas has a dark coloring, similar to the men in black at a garden party. The hats are so cheerful, the audience may be misled. Your breasts meanwhile cast a spell, and swell, almost big enough to lift me. I enjoy your legs. There is a time for that, a little clearing in the woods, a sunspot, a capsule in the gloom, which gets me thinking my being can become something else, something happier and lighter, as if my planetary influence were flight and not these footprints. The lift-off is temporary. The rain keeps falling, at various speeds, with various thicknesses, some of them nearly unbearable, and I am huddled at the foot of a tree, wanting you to lift me, wanting you to go away. Such a bare, forked animal I am, and somehow lost, somehow off the path. There are degrees of nakedness. I am still a young man, an actor of manhood, in fact, and I cannot say which degree of nakedness is suitable for the occasion. I would compose myself, if I knew how. I would be more elevated, or more plain, give you more art or less rope. You suspect, perhaps, that mine is a hopeless case. You can purloin me and get nowhere. It's not me. In person, none of my parts, none of my stances, none of my looks represents me. On paper, the same; none of my confessions or allusions stand up to the flesh. I am full of wishes that do not recognize each other, and moods that come from different spirits. I wear motley, and good will never come of motley. I mistake what I'm feeling as I mistake what you're feeling, which leaves us forever in the dark, befuddled or rapturous, but never at peace. It may be that the slit in your sarong and the slit in my cape are all we know, and cannot tell, of marriage.

# Self-Portrait as Egg White

The burner makes me presentable; it gives me a sun, and I circle the sun.

What a form of worship, and then, what fantastic moorings!

At room temperature, my world is without form. The flame makes it a perfect ring, and light swims all around the ring.

* * *

Look at my ducklings. And look at my swordfish.

# *Sizing*

Size, I mean a thing like Chicago's politics or Churchill's appetites, is a rare quantity. I have a big nose, which Freud thought a sign of sexual well-being, and big ears, which the Japanese attribute to wise men. But I am really a little man, anxious, and easily disturbed. I may publish little poems in little magazines, hoping to build stature, but I know my days of inferiority cannot be numbered.

Psychologically, my eagerness for bigness has become the strongest proof of my littleness. I cannot accept the transcendental view that all lives are equally big, or rather, equally little; that no one should suffer in the presence of other humans, since the enlargement and reduction of other humans is a dream of the self, which the self vainly takes for real. Thus I reason with myself.

But I cannot find the dream in my life. I may only note it, at one remove. I've yet to experience a true scale, one free of human impulse and inhuman exaggeration. Until then, I will always be restless, trapped between little and big. For all the little things I accept (my little rooms, my little prayers of devotion), I am more aware of my failure to see the big things, the miracles, the nights of the winegrower.

My heart is little, and hardly moves.

# First Confession

I am bluer, deeper, and emptier than the sky—this will be inscribed on wooden blocks—I am lost, I am immaterial—it will be written in dirt—I make every sail a night-sail, and shadow every patio, and seek the honor of drowning—the wind will no longer be clear, it will darken whatever it blows on; the fossil record will be destroyed; the surveys, charts, astronomer's charts, space-ash, evidence—one spring is all it takes, and one fall—I pull at my father's beard, and I'm cut from my father's eyes—this will be scribbled in chalk—*In a dark dark wood, there was a dark dark place, and in that dark dark place, was a dark dark room—storks are enchanted men—parks are enchanted women—they dream together, apart, on opposite sides of a huge round stone*—it will be placed in notebooks—I am changed, I'm neuter, I am impotent and omnipotent—this hundred-armed goddess, that blind Greek—a horoscope interrupts the horizon line—tracks it all the way to the sea, right into the brood of mountainsides—and midnight still belongs to midnight—it's midnight's gardens, midnight's windows and cells and drippings and predictions, midnight's well-urine and kitchen-milk—I am a tourist in them—a tourist in the horoscope—squinting, lost, decompassed, hungry—hugely and vaguely hungry—all of this will be hid in wooden clocks, it will be penned in leather-bound books—I am bluer, deeper, and emptier than the sky—I'm waiting for you—

# Self-Portrait as Grand Hotel

I reside in this Palladium of yellow brick; this Pythagoras of onyx columns; this den of candelabras; this forest of wall hangings—all stags, lilies, pear trees—from the days of the Sun King. I come to this land of staircases; of jet-veined rock; of ornately carved frogs and brass railings; of chandeliers with an unprecedented heaviness, which cast an unprecedented light; of carpets whose intricate, myth-ridden patterns are too deep for unraveling. I reside amidst Greek, Nubian, Copt, and Mameluk artifacts, all under glass; Kashmiri trees, with their flashing leaves and tight, winding stems; zebrawood settees with bronze finials and Ambertique cushions; windows with an Arabesque look; halls with gas-lamps and cherubim. Every morning, I sit at a desk made of olive bark, on a balcony swimming with frangipani. I, too, become overwhelmingly lush, sensual, cultured, the last representative of an English-speaking world, not about to be demolished.

## Credo

I am the tool-using animal (homo faber), the social animal (zoon politikon), and a man. I bring my hammer. My lips are wet and round. But you hide in another box, lower and deeper than the world. That box has a massive lid, which homo faber cannot pry, and zoon politikon cannot see. At bottom, I am not thoughtful. I know that the peanut butter will not be where I put it today, nor the umbrella where I put it tomorrow. I cannot make love like zoon politikon, or build a summer house like homo faber. But I use the language well. I love my wife. And I keep asking.

*doorway for the house*

each other, one another, an object to complete our meaning, myself and yourself, ourselves, a doorway for the house, for itself, who plans to hold us, who holds us, the house, I made a doorway for the house, you came in the house and lay in the sun, these days, yourself, themselves, these days of yours, lying in the sun at three, you and the sun, the light that, of which, I know, an object to complete you, when I see you, half-dressed, in the sun at three, unconscious of myself, those days being pushed from the house, who holds us now, not me and not you, yet each other and one another, whoever comes in, stands in the doorway, makes speech, speech itself in the doorway, and sky itself in the doorway, one another, between themselves, between us, between the cloth and the body, the thing that modifies and the thing that lives, love is given, it shows, it shows itself to the house, to the animals in the house and the inanimate objects, to the persons and the short and long syllables, love is a given, love adds to us, we add to it, to complete its meaning, ours, standing in the doorway, in the larger light from the street and the smaller light from the hall, at three in the afternoon, with everything still to say, suffering to complete our meaning, ourselves, that love and its pronouns keep returning.

## After Supper

Another human being with large toenails and deep-set eyes slides under the comforter, sighs once or twice, and takes up last night's story.

The train passes the old mill ... A dog returns from the store without his owner ... The field of cicadas raises its voice ...

Minutes later, a woman removes her button-down shirt with one hand, and moves in, solemnly.

She brings the final pyramid of moonlit grapes.

# ABOUT THE AUTHOR

Brian Johnson is the author of *Self-Portrait*. His poems have appeared in many journals, including *American Letters & Commentary*, *West Branch*, *Quarter after Eight*, *Sentence*, *Drunken Boat*, and *North Dakota Quarterly*. The recipient of a Connecticut Commission on the Arts Fellowship and two Pushcart Prize nominations, he teaches composition and creative writing at Southern Connecticut State University.